THIS BOO{}
BELONGS {}

Name: Age:

Favourite player:

2020/2021

My Predictions...   Actual...

The Rams' final position:

The Rams' top scorer:

Championship winners:

Championship top scorer:

FA Cup winners:

EFL Cup winners:

Contributors: Peter Rogers

A TWOCAN PUBLICATION

©2020. Published by twocan under licence from Derby County Football Club.

ISBN: 978-1-913362-28-7

£9

CONTENTS

DAVID 01 MARSHALL

POSITION: Goalkeeper **DOB:** 05/03/1985
COUNTRY: Scotland

Following his summer arrival from Wigan Athletic, Scotland international goalkeeper David Marshall brings a wealth of Championship, Premier League and international experience to the Derby County dressing room.

The former Celtic, Norwich, Cardiff and Hull 'keeper is a commanding presence and fantastic shot stopper who is sure to provide great competition for the No1 spot at Pride Park in 2020/21.

02 ANDRE WISDOM

POSITION: Defender **DOB:** 09/05/1993
COUNTRY: England

The 2020/21 campaign will be defender Andre Wisdom's fourth consecutive season with the Rams, in what is his second spell at the club.

Wisdom first joined the Rams from Liverpool on a season-long loan deal in 2013/14. He also gained further first team experience when the Anfield club loaned him to West Bromwich Albion, Norwich City and Red Bull Salzburg. The former England under-21 international then completed a permanent switch to Derby in July 2017.

CRAIG 03 FORSYTH

POSITION: Defender **DOB:** 24/02/1989
COUNTRY: Scotland

Scotland international Craig Forsyth is one of the Rams' longest-serving players among the current squad. The versatile defender, who can also operate in midfield, began his career with Dundee and joined Derby from Watford in 2013.

Forsyth initially arrived at Pride Park on loan from the Hornets in March 2013 and after impressing across a ten-game spell, he then completed a £150,000 permanent move to the club in July 2013. He has now played over 200 games for the Rams.

GRAEME 04 SHINNIE

POSITION: Midfielder **DOB:** 04/08/1991
COUNTRY: Scotland

Another Scotland international among the ranks at Pride Park, midfielder Graeme Shinnie joined the club from Aberdeen in July 2019.

After agreeing a three-year deal with the Rams, Shinnie made his Derby debut in the EFL Cup victory at Scunthorpe the following month. His first goal for the Rams was a dramatic injury-time winner against Wigan Athletic in October 2019. In total the 29-year-old Scot featured in 27 games in 2019/20, scoring twice.

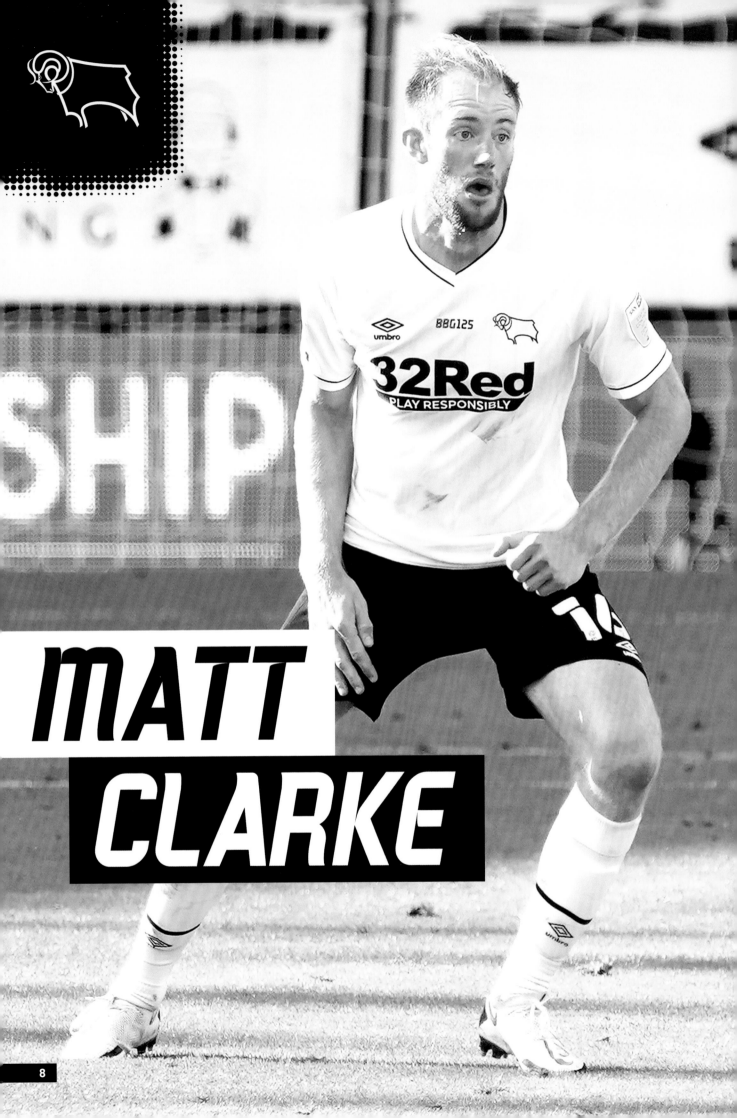

MATT
CLARKE

SOCCER SKILLS

Great goalkeepers are an essential ingredient for successful teams in today's game. They have to excel in all areas of the art of 'keeping and David Marshall is a great 'keeper that lives up to these expectations.

DISTRIBUTION
THE BASICS OF GOOD THROWING TECHNIQUE

OVERARM THROW

This is best for covering long distances. The body should be in line with the direction of the throw with the weight on the back foot. The ball should be brought forward in a bowling action with the arm straight.

JAVELIN THROW

This throw is made quickly with a low trajectory. The arm is bent for this throw, the ball is held beside the head and the body is in line with the direction of the throw. The arm is brought forward in a pushing movement with the ball being released at the top.

UNDERARM THROW

The ball is released from a crouching position, with a smooth underarm swing.

Throws do not usually travel as far as kicks but the greater speed and accuracy of throwing can make up for the lack of distance and will help the team retain possession. A player receiving a throw must be able to control it early.

Work hard at distribution and the benefits of this will be seen whenever you are in possession during a match.

EXERCISE ONE

Grab a friend and throw the ball to each other using the various throwing techniques at various distances apart.

EXERCISE TWO

The goalkeeper with the ball uses the various throws to knock another ball off a marker.

EXERCISE THREE

The goalkeepers try to throw the ball through the markers using various throwing techniques.

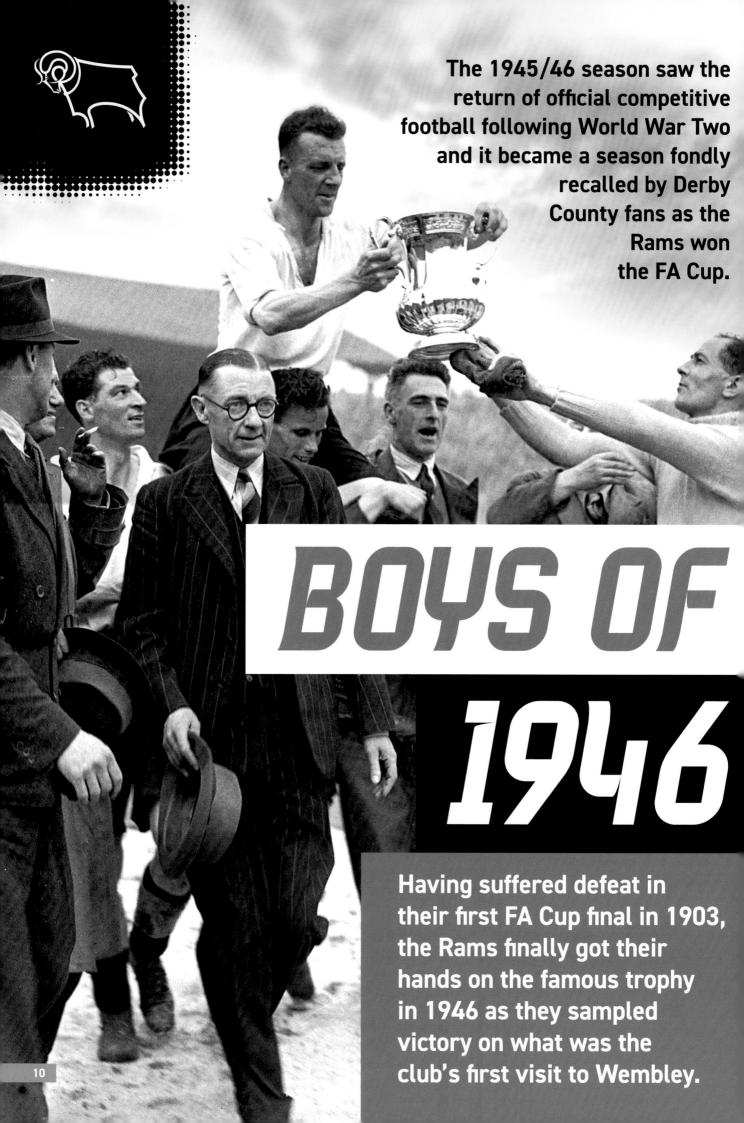

The 1945/46 season saw the return of official competitive football following World War Two and it became a season fondly recalled by Derby County fans as the Rams won the FA Cup.

BOYS OF 1946

Having suffered defeat in their first FA Cup final in 1903, the Rams finally got their hands on the famous trophy in 1946 as they sampled victory on what was the club's first visit to Wembley.

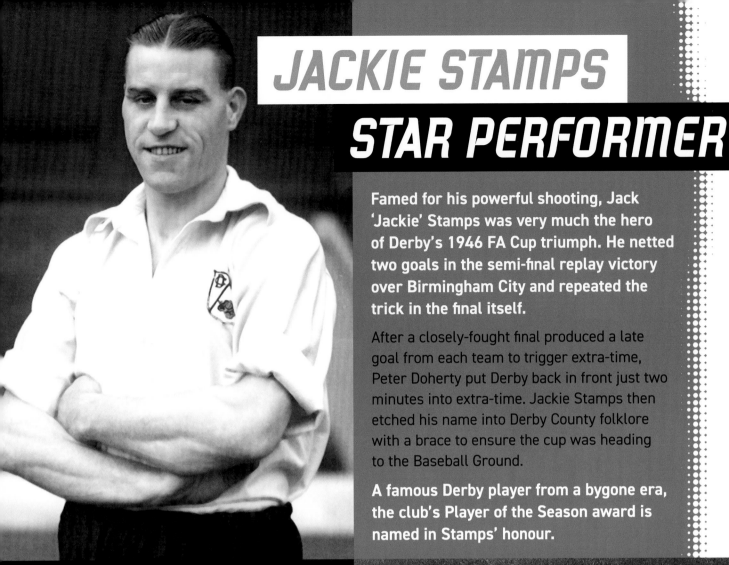

JACKIE STAMPS

STAR PERFORMER

Famed for his powerful shooting, Jack 'Jackie' Stamps was very much the hero of Derby's 1946 FA Cup triumph. He netted two goals in the semi-final replay victory over Birmingham City and repeated the trick in the final itself.

After a closely-fought final produced a late goal from each team to trigger extra-time, Peter Doherty put Derby back in front just two minutes into extra-time. Jackie Stamps then etched his name into Derby County folklore with a brace to ensure the cup was heading to the Baseball Ground.

A famous Derby player from a bygone era, the club's Player of the Season award is named in Stamps' honour.

Derby began their cup crusade with a two-legged third-round tie with Luton Town which they comfortably won 9-0 on aggregate. The fourth and fifth rounds were also played over two legs and saw the Rams defeat West Bromwich Albion 1-0 and 3-1 before cruising past Brighton & Hove Albion 10-1 on aggregate with 4-1 and 6-0 victories.

The quarter-finals were again two-legged affairs and saw Derby edge past Aston Villa 5-4 over the two games. Birmingham City provided the semi-final opposition and after an initial 1-1 draw at Hillsborough, Derby won a Maine Road replay 4-0.

A dramatic end to the final saw Derby take an 85th-minute lead when Dally Duncan's shot deflected off of Bert Turner and past Charlton 'keeper Sam Bartram. Amazingly, the Addicks levelled almost straight from the restart and extra-time beckoned.

The additional period saw goals from Peter Doherty and a Jackie Stamps brace win the day for the Rams before skipper Jack Nicholls led his team up the famous Wembley steps to collect the trophy as Derby County began the post-war era in the best possible way.

MIKE 06
TE WIERIK

POSITION: Defender   DOB: 08/06/1992
COUNTRY: Holland

In February 2020 the Rams announced they had agreed terms with Groningen captain Mike te Wierik to join the club in the summer.

The central defender made his debut in the Rams' EFL Cup match with Barrow at Pride Park and impressed with his defensive performance and his leadership qualities which boss Phillip Cocu believes will be of great benefit to the squad during the 2020/21 campaign.

05 KRYSTIAN
BIELIK

POSITION: Midfielder   DOB: 04/01/1998
COUNTRY: Poland

Poland international Krystian Bielik joined Derby County on a five-year deal from Arsenal in August 2019.

With the ability to perform in midfield or in central defence, the Pole had enjoyed an excellent 2018/19 campaign while on loan at Charlton Athletic where he helped the Addicks win promotion to the Championship. His maiden season at Derby saw him make 21 appearances for Phillips Cocu's side before suffering a knee injury in January 2020 which ended his season.

KAMIL 07 JÓŹWIAK

POSITION: Striker **DOB:** 22/04/1998
COUNTRY: Poland

Derby County strengthened their attacking options with the signing of Poland international wideman Kamil Jóźwiak in September 2020.

The 22-year-old winger joined the Rams from Polish top-flight side Lech Poznan for an undisclosed fee and signed a four-year deal. He made his Derby debut away to Luton Town and tasted his first victory in a Rams shirt in the 1-0 win away to Norwich City in October 2020.

MAX 08 BIRD

POSITION: Midfielder **DOB:** 18/09/2000
COUNTRY: England

Another product of the Rams' successful youth Academy, midfielder Max Bird really established himself on the first team scene in the second half of the 2019/20 season.

After enjoying a first team debut back in September 2017 in an EFL Cup tie, Bird made a total of 27 appearances in all competitions last season and will look to continue his first team involvement in 2020/21.

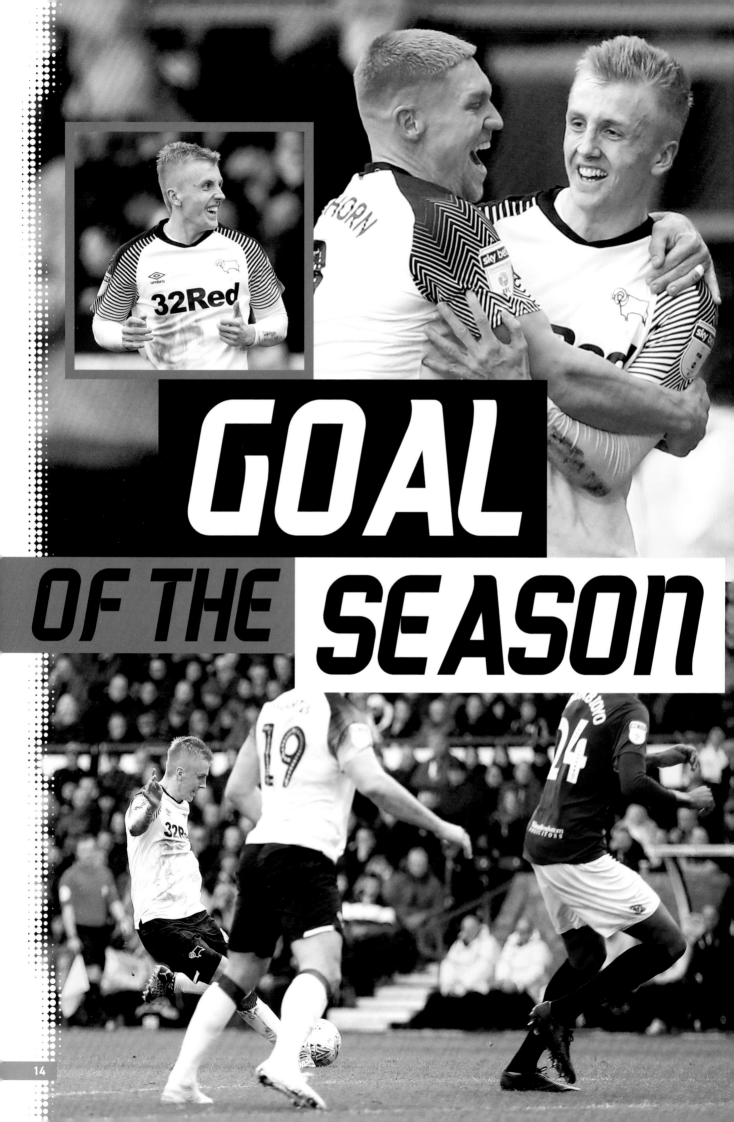

GOAL
OF THE SEASON

LOUIE SIBLEY

V BLACKBURN ROVERS

MARCH 2020

Louie Sibley's stunning strike against Blackburn Rovers at Pride Park in March 2020 was voted Derby County's Goal of the Season and capped of a memorable breakthrough campaign for the exciting youngster. What made the goal even more impressive was that it came 26 minutes into his first league start for the Rams.

Fed the ball by striker Martyn Waghorn, the highly-rated midfielder took a touch and fired the ball into the top corner, leaving Blackburn goalkeeper Christian Walton with no chance. The teenager's effort put the Rams ahead against Rovers before a brace from Chris Martin secured a 3-0 win and a valuable three points.

Sibley's strike beat off competition from Tom Lawrence's strike against Huddersfield Town, Graeme Shinnie's half volley against Wigan Athletic and Wayne Rooney's free-kick against Stoke City, following a supporters' vote.

The award was Sibley's second of the season after the Academy product also landed the club's Scholar of the Season accolade. These two high-profile awards capped off a campaign which saw an impressive rise for the talented teenager, who made his debut for the club against Scunthorpe United in the first round of the Carabao Cup in August 2019.

His first league appearance came just before Christmas against Reading. He appeared off the bench in a defeat at the Madejski Stadium and continued to impress and excel in the club's under-23 side.

He started in the FA Cup encounters against Crystal Palace, Northampton Town and Manchester United, winning the Man of the Match award against the Red Devils at Pride Park. That led to his first start of the season against Blackburn Rovers at Pride Park in the last fixture before the coronavirus outbreak.

The break could have halted his progress, however, once football resumed in June, he picked up from where he left off, scoring his first senior hat-trick in a 3-2 victory against Millwall at the Den.

Assists followed for Sibley in games against Reading and Cardiff City, whilst he scored his fifth goal of the season in the final league game of the season in a 3-1 victory over Birmingham City at St Andrew's.

Challenge your favourite grown-up and find out which of you is the biggest Championship brain!

ADULTS

Who is the only Championship club to have won the Premier League?

1 ANSWER

How many teams in the 2020/21 Championship have never competed in the Premier League?

2 ANSWER

Which former Leeds United and Norwich City midfielder currently plays for Middlesbrough?

3 ANSWER

At which Scottish club was QPR manager Mark Warburton once in charge?

4 ANSWER

Blackburn Rovers' manager Tony Mowbray previously played for and managed which Championship rival?

5 ANSWER

At which club did Sheffield Wednesday manager Garry Monk begin his managerial career?

6 ANSWER

From which club did Boro sign striker Britt Assombalonga?

7 ANSWER

Millwall manager Gary Rowett previously played for the Lions - true or false?

8 ANSWER

At which Championship ground will you find the Invincibles Stand?

9 ANSWER

In which year did Steve Cooper become Swansea City manager?

10 ANSWER

16

V KIDS

The adults' questions are on the left page and the kids' questions are on the right page.

ANSWERS ON PAGE 62

Which Championship club play their home games at Carrow Road?

1 ANSWER

What is Sheffield Wednesday's nickname?

2 ANSWER

Which two clubs won automatic promotion to the Championship in 2019/20?

3 ANSWER

Ashton Gate is home to which Championship club?

4

Who is the manager of Cardiff City?

5

How many Welsh clubs are competing in the 2020/21 Championship?

6 ANSWER

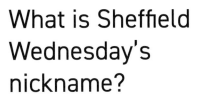

Mark Warburton is the manager of which Championship team?

7 ANSWER

Which Championship stadium has the largest capacity?

8

How many Championship clubs have the word 'City' in their name?

9 ANSWER

What nationality is Preston manager Alex Neil?

10

Fill the page with your footy goals and dreams, no matter how big or small, and then start working on how to accomplish them!

We've started you off...

1. Visit Pride Park

2. Complete 50 keepy-uppies

FOOTY BUCKET LIST

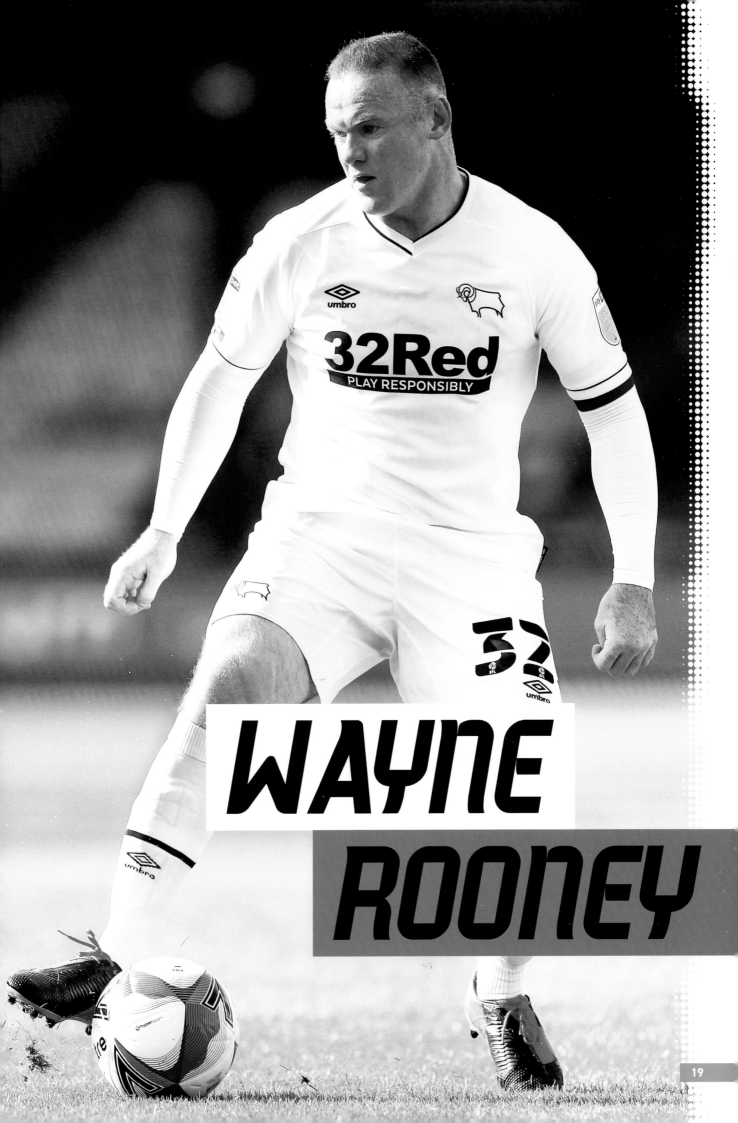

WAYNE
ROONEY

WHO ARE YER?

Can you figure out the identity of all these Rams stars?

ANSWERS ON PAGE 62

10 TOM LAWRENCE

POSITION: Midfielder **DOB:** 13/01/1994
COUNTRY: Wales

A full Wales international, midfielder Tom Lawrence joined the Rams from Midlands rivals Leicester City in August 2017 having taken in a number of loan spells while with the Foxes.

A real attack-minded midfielder who loves to get forward and score goals, he bagged a brace as Derby began their 2019/20 season with a 2-1 win at Huddersfield Town. He went on to hit double figures for the season and ended the campaign with ten goals.

09 MARTYN WAGHORN

POSITION: Striker **DOB:** 23/03/1990
COUNTRY: England

Recruited from Ipswich Town in the summer of 2017, striker Martyn Waghorn has become a key member of the Derby County squad.

He featured in 47 games last season and netted 12 goals including a brace in the Rams' 2-2 draw at Stoke in August 2019. Waghorn's goalscoring prowess and phenomenal work-rate have made him a popular character with his teammates and among the club's fan base.

11 JORDON IBE

POSITION: Forward **DOB:** 08/12/1995
COUNTRY: England

The Rams added another attacking option to their squad by completing the signing of winger Jordon Ibe in September 2020.

He joined Derby as a free agent after leaving AFC Bournemouth. Ibe is certainly no stranger to Derby fans after he impressed during a loan spell from Premier League giants Liverpool during the 2014/15 campaign.

Derby supporters will once again be excited to see the former England under-21 man produce his trickery at Pride Park Stadium in 2020/21.

12 NATHAN BYRNE

POSITION: Defender **DOB:** 05/06/1992
COUNTRY: England

Derby County swooped for Wigan Athletic right-back Nathan Byrne on the eve of the new 2020/21 Sky Bet Championship season.

An experienced EFL campaigner, Byrne will provide boss Phillip Cocu with further full-back options following Jayden Bogle's move to Premier League Sheffield United. Byrne has made over 300 career appearances and is a defender who enjoys making an impact when going forward to support the attack.

PREPARING FOR ACTION

Football matches may well be scheduled for 90 minutes but there are many days of preparation that go into making sure that Phillip Cocu's men are at their physical and mental peak when they cross the white line to represent Derby County Football Club.

Like all Championship clubs, the Rams' pre-match planning is meticulous. The manager of course has final say as to who makes his starting line-up but the boss is ably assisted by a backroom staff of coaches, sports scientists, strength and conditioning experts, physiotherapists and nutritionists who all play their part in helping fine tune the players ahead of the manager's team selection.

The majority of the squads' preparations take place at the club's training ground and that all begins when the players report back for pre-season training.

Although the modern-day player has little down-time in terms of maintaining his overall fitness, pre-season really is a vital time for footballers to build themselves up to remain as fit, strong and healthy as possible for the challenging season that awaits.

The pre-season schedule often begins with a series of fitness tests. The results of those tests enables the club's coaching and fitness staff to assess each player's condition and level of fitness to ensure they are given the right work load during the pre-season programme.

When it comes to winning football matches, it is well known that both hard work and practice are two essential ingredients to success. However, in terms of strength and fitness, then rest, recovery and diet also have crucial parts to play in a footballer's wellbeing.

The modern game now sees technology playing its part in training too - prior to beginning their training sessions, the players are provided with a GPS tracking system and heart rate analysis monitors ensuring that all that they do in a training session can be measured, monitored and reviewed.

On-pitch training drills and gym work is now enhanced further with players often taking part in yoga and pilates classes while always receiving expert advice in terms of their diet, rest and mental welfare.

JACK
MARRIOTT

SOCCER SKILLS
DEFENDING

Defending is an art - not as spectacular as swerving a free kick around the wall into the net or floating a crossfield pass into the path of an oncoming wingback - but nevertheless, just as important. Every successful team has a solid defence and can defend as a team.

Defenders must also master the art of defending one on one...

EXERCISE ONE

Two adjacent 10m x 10m grids have two players, X and Y at the opposite ends of the grids. X plays the ball to Y, who is then allowed to attack defender X with the ball. Y's target is to be able to stop the ball, under control, on the opposite end line. Defender X has to try to stop this happening. Y is encouraged to be direct and run at X with the ball.

KEY FACTORS

1. Do not approach the attacker square on. Adopt a sideways stance which enables rapid forward and backwards movement.

2. Do not dive in. Be patient and wait for your opponent to make a mistake. Always be on your toes.

3. Threaten the ball without actually committing to a tackle. Pretending to tackle can often panic the opponent!

4. Tackle when you are sure you will win it!

EXERCISE TWO

Here the game is progressed to a two v two situation when X1 and X2 play as a team against Y1 and Y2.

The same target is used for this game - the players have to stand on the opposite line with the ball, either by dribbling past their opponents or by passing the ball through them.

The same key factors are relevant here with the addition of two more:

5. Covering your defending partner when he is being attacked.

6. Communication between the two defenders is vital.

If a team can get these points of defending right, throughout the side, they will become very difficult to beat.

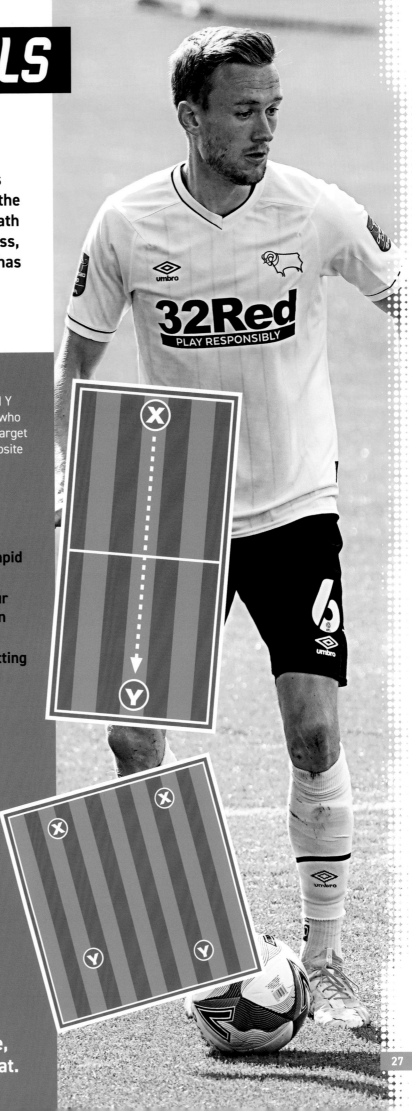

WHICH FOOTBALLER
ARE YOU?

1. What is your favourite activity at the park?

a. Leaping around

b. Practicing my heading

c. Lots of non-stop running

d. Scoring goals

2. What is your biggest strength?

a. My height

b. My strength

c. My stamina

d. My speed

3. Which would you rather win?

a. A game of catch

b. A weight lifting contest

c. A long distance run

d. A sprint race

4. You score a goal! How do you celebrate?

a. I turn and punch the air

b. I clench my fist in delight

c. I high-five a teammate

d. I slide on my knees

5. How would the opposition describe you?

a. Hard to beat

b. Determined to succeed

c. All-action

d. Lethal in front of goal

6. What's your favourite move?

a. Springing high to catch under pressure

b. A sliding tackle

c. Playing the perfect through ball

d. Spinning away from my marker

7. What is the key to winning a game?

a. Keeping a clean sheet

b. Winning your individual battles

c. Maintaining possession

d. Taking chances that come your way

8. What is your favourite number?

a. One

b. Five

c. Seven

d. Nine

9. How would you describe your style of play?

a. Disciplined

b. Fully committed

c. Relentless

d. Technically gifted

10. What do your teammates call you?

a. Secure

b. Reliable

c. Energetic

d. Mr/Miss goals

MOSTLY As

You would clearly be a safe pair of hands in goal. Watch out David Marshall, there's competition for the No1 shirt!

MOSTLY Bs

Sounds like you are a young Andre Wisdom in the making - there could well be a role for you in the Rams back four...

MOSTLY Cs

You could comfortably take your place in the heart of midfield and help make things tick at Pride Park. Move over Max Bird!

MOSTLY Ds

Looks like we have a budding Kamil Jóźwiak on our hands! Who do you fancy partnering in attack?

JACK 14 MARRIOTT

POSITION: Striker **DOB:** 09/09/1994
COUNTRY: England

The hero of the Rams' 2018/19 Play-Off semi-final triumph over Leeds United at Elland Road, lively striker Jack Marriott featured in 37 games for Phillip Cocu's side in 2019/20.

An experienced frontman, Marriott began his career with Ipswich Town before rising to prominence with impressive goals-to-games spells with Luton Town and Peterborough United - he joined the Rams in the summer of 2018.

MATT 16 CLARKE

POSITION: Defender **DOB:** 22/09/1996
COUNTRY: England

Derby County were delighted to secure the services of central defender Matt Clarke on loan from Brighton & Hove Albion for a second successive season ahead of the 2020/21 campaign.

Such was Clarke's form during his initial loan spell at Pride Park in 2019/20 that he ended the season by landing the Jack Stamps Player of the Season award. He made 37 appearances last season and is sure to be one of the first names on Phillip Cocu's teamsheet in 2020/21.

TEAM 2020/21

LOUIE 17 SIBLEY

POSITION: Midfielder   **DOB:** 13/09/2001
COUNTRY: England

Having initially joined the Rams' Academy as an under-8, Louie Sibley burst onto the first team scene in 2019/20.

An attacking midfielder who certainly has an eye for goal, Sibley marked his full Championship debut with a goal against Blackburn Rovers – a strike that was later voted the Rams' Goal of the Season. After netting a memorable hat-trick in the 3-2 win away to Millwall in June, Sibley ended the season by landing the club's Scholar of the Year award.

BOYS OF
1972

Derby County and their loyal supporters were certainly given a nail-biting end to the club's memorable 1971/72 season. Under the inspirational management of Brian Clough and Peter Taylor, Derby produced some scintillating football during a three-way battle with Leeds United and Liverpool for the First Division title.

As the season reached it conclusion, Derby lifted the Texaco Cup with a 2-1 second-leg victory over Airdrieonians on 26 April 1971. The Rams then completed their First Division fixtures at home to Liverpool five days later.

COLIN BOULTON

STAR PERFORMER

It is no secret that behind any successful team is a top quality goalkeeper. Although others may have grabbed the headlines in the Rams' 1971/72 First Division title-winning campaign, goalkeeper Colin Boulton provided the vital clean sheets that so many victories were built upon.

When the Rams defeated West Ham United 2-0 in August 1971, the match saw Boulton record his first clean sheet of the season. The ever-present No1 proceeded to record a further 22 league shut-outs in 42 matches as Derby landed top spot.

Words such as 'solid' and 'dependable' are often used by his former teammates when reflecting upon Boulton's contribution to the club's success in the 1970s. His reliability and consistency in the Rams' goal in 1971/72 can certainly never be underestimated and in 2009 he was voted as being Derby Country's greatest ever goalkeeper.

John McGovern's second-half goal proved enough to give Derby both points and leave Clough's title-chasing team top of the table having completed their 42-fixture programme. However, due to postponements earlier in the season, title-rivals Liverpool and Leeds United both had a final game still to play.

Seven days on from the Baseball Ground triumph over Liverpool and the waiting was finally over. Liverpool, who needed to win to overtake the Rams, were held to a goalless draw against Arsenal at Highbury, while Leeds United suffered a 2-1 defeat away to Wolverhampton Wanderers. So without even having to kick a ball, Derby County Football Club were crowned First Division champions!

This was an outstanding achievement for the club as it celebrated a first Division One title and the accolade of being the finest team in the land. The Rams would also look forward to the prospect of European football coming to the Baseball Ground in 1972/73.

COLOUR
JASON
KNIGHT

MIKE
TE WIERIK

PLAYER
OF THE SEASON

MATT CLARKE

Central defender Matt Clarke capped off a highly impressive season on loan at Pride Park by being crowned the Jack Stamps Player of the Season for the 2019/20 campaign. The 24-year-old, who joined the Rams on a season-long loan from Premier League side Brighton & Hove Albion in August 2019, became only the second loan player to win the award after he followed in the footsteps of Chelsea loanee Fikayo Tomori who landed the award in 2018/19.

The award, voted for by the club's supporters, was given to the defender following a fine campaign for Derby when he made 37 appearances in all competitions after debuting in the Rams' opening night 2-1 victory away to Huddersfield Town.

Despite his role primarily being to help prevent the opposition from scoring, Clarke also added his name to the scoresheet when he netted the only goal of the game to seal a 1-0 home victory over Hull City in January 2020. However, it was his consistent performances at the back under manager Phillip Cocu which set him apart during the season as he swiftly established himself as a key player at the heart of the defence.

Whilst he had to adapt his game to suit the style Cocu wanted his side to play, he remained solid and consistent in his performances which led the Rams to a late charge for the Sky Bet Championship Play-Off positions.

In August 2020 the club were delighted to have secured Clarke's services from the Seagulls again for 2020/21 and will be hoping for he can carry on from where he left off last season.

YOUNG PLAYER OF THE SEASON

LOUIE SIBLEY

Rising through the Rams' Academy since joining as an under-8, attacking midfielder Louie Sibley capped off a memorable 2019/20 campaign by being named the club's Scholar of the Season.

The 2019/20 season proved to be a breakthrough campaign for Sibley who made his first team debut in the Rams' EFL Cup victory away to Scunthorpe United in August 2019. He then marked his first Championship start with a stunning goal against Blackburn Rovers in March 2020 before grabbing the headlines with a hat-trick against Millwall.

After making 17 first team appearances in 2019/20 and scoring five goals, all eyes will be on the teenage sensation in 2020/21 and beyond.

MORGAN 18 WHITTAKER

POSITION: Striker **DOB:** 07/01/2001
COUNTRY: England

An England youth international, striker Morgan Whittaker forms part of an exciting crop of young players who made their mark on the Rams' first team in 2019/20.

Whittaker netted his first goal for the club as Derby County concluded their 2019/20 campaign with a 3-1 victory over Birmingham City. The teenage forward also make a bright start to the new season when he slotted home the winning penalty in the EFL Cup shoot-out victory over Barrow on the opening day of the season.

KELLE 21 ROOS

POSITION: Goalkeeper **DOB:** 31/05/1992
COUNTRY: Netherlands

Dutch 'keeper Kelle Roos has been with the Rams since early 2014 and gained valuable first team experience with a series of loan spells before breaking into the Derby team during the memorable 2018/19 campaign.

Roos' first appearance of the 2020/21 season saw him become the hero of the hour with a string of fine penalty saves as the Rams overcame league new boys Barrow in the first round of the EFL Cup in September.

22 GEORGE EVANS

POSITION: Midfielder **DOB:** 13/12/1994
COUNTRY: England

A versatile performer, who can operate in either defence or midfield, George Evans became one of former manager Frank Lampard's first signings as Derby County boss when he arrived at Pride Park from Championship rivals Reading in the summer of 2018.

Injuries have hampered his progress at Derby but in 2019/20 he enjoyed 20 appearances under the management of Phillip Cocu and is certainly a valuable member of the Rams' squad.

CLASSIC
FANTASTIC

There are five Rammies hiding in the crowd as Derby fans celebrate the Rams winning the Championship Play-Off final and promotion to the Premier League in 2007. **Can you find him?**

ANSWERS ON PAGE 62

41

GRAEME
SHINNIE

Can you find the eight differences between these two photos?

SPOT THE DIFFERENCE

ANSWERS ON PAGE 62

Here are our predictions for the 2020/21 season, see if you agree!

2020/21

PREMIER LEAGUE

OUR PREDICTION FOR PREMIER LEAGUE WINNERS:
LEICESTER CITY

YOUR PREDICTION:

OUR PREDICTION FOR PREMIER LEAGUE RUNNERS-UP:
LIVERPOOL

YOUR PREDICTION:

CHAMPIONSHIP

OUR PREDICTION FOR CHAMPIONSHIP WINNERS:
DERBY COUNTY

YOUR PREDICTION:

OUR PREDICTION FOR CHAMPIONSHIP RUNNERS-UP:
SWANSEA CITY

YOUR PREDICTION:

TOP SCORERS

OUR PREDICTION FOR PREMIER LEAGUE TOP SCORER:

PIERRE-EMERICK AUBAMEYANG

YOUR PREDICTION:

OUR PREDICTION FOR CHAMPIONSHIP TOP SCORER:

KAMIL JÓŹWIAK

YOUR PREDICTION:

FA CUP & EFL CUP

OUR PREDICTION FOR FA CUP WINNERS:

BRIGHTON & HA

YOUR PREDICTION:

OUR PREDICTION FOR EFL CUP WINNERS:

MIDDLESBROUGH

YOUR PREDICTION:

PREDICTIONS

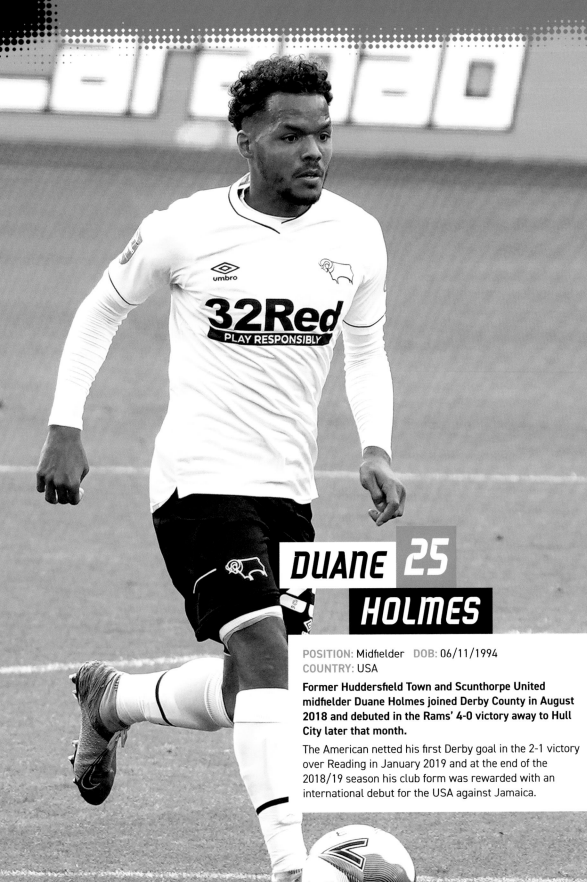

DUANE 25 HOLMES

POSITION: Midfielder   **DOB:** 06/11/1994
COUNTRY: USA

Former Huddersfield Town and Scunthorpe United midfielder Duane Holmes joined Derby County in August 2018 and debuted in the Rams' 4-0 victory away to Hull City later that month.

The American netted his first Derby goal in the 2-1 victory over Reading in January 2019 and at the end of the 2018/19 season his club form was rewarded with an international debut for the USA against Jamaica.

26 LEE BUCHANAN

POSITION: Defender **DOB:** 07/03/2001
COUNTRY: England

Having joined the Rams' Academy at under-14 level, Lee Buchanan has progressed through the age groups and into the first team squad.

The left-sided defender made great strides in 2018/19 with both the under-18 and under-23 sides before being elevated to the first team bench in January 2019. Buchanan has since clearly caught the eye of Phillip Cocu who handed the youngster his first team debut against Scunthopre United in the 2019/20 EFL Cup.

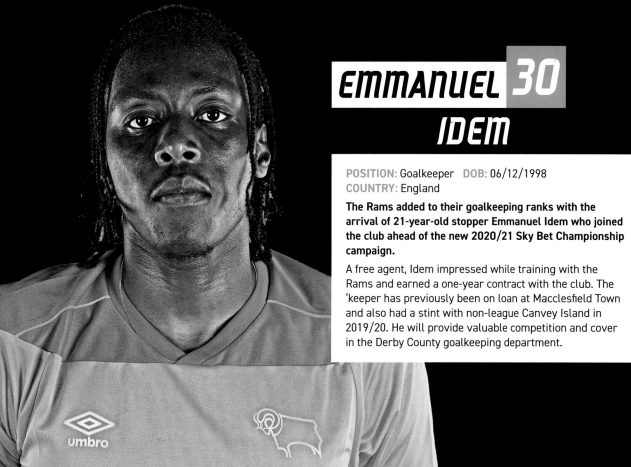

EMMANUEL 30 IDEM

POSITION: Goalkeeper **DOB:** 06/12/1998
COUNTRY: England

The Rams added to their goalkeeping ranks with the arrival of 21-year-old stopper Emmanuel Idem who joined the club ahead of the new 2020/21 Sky Bet Championship campaign.

A free agent, Idem impressed while training with the Rams and earned a one-year contract with the club. The 'keeper has previously been on loan at Macclesfield Town and also had a stint with non-league Canvey Island in 2019/20. He will provide valuable competition and cover in the Derby County goalkeeping department.

KAMIL
JÓŹWIAK

SOCCER SKILLS
CHEST CONTROL

Controlling the ball quickly and with minimum fuss in order to get the ball where you want it, so you can pass or shoot, can be the difference between a good player and a top class player.

EXERCISE ONE

Grab two of your mates to start the exercise. A and C stand 10yds apart and have a ball each, ready to act as servers.

B works first. B must run towards A who serves the ball for B to control with the chest and pass back to A. B then turns, runs to C and repeats the exercise.

Once B has worked for 30 seconds all the players rotate.

KEY FACTORS

1. Look to control the ball as early as possible.
2. Get in line with the ball.
3. Keep eyes on the ball.
4. Relax the body on impact with the ball to cushion it.

EXERCISE TWO

In this exercise there are 5 servers positioned around a 15yd square. At one side of the square there is a goal.

T starts in the middle of the square. S1 serves first, throwing the ball in the air towards T. T must control the ball with the chest and try to shoot past the goalkeeper, as soon as T has shot on goal they must prepare for the next serve from S2.

Once T has received a ball from every server the players rotate positions - the same key factors apply.

Players who can control a ball quickly, putting the ball in a position for a shot or pass, give themselves and their teammates the extra valuable seconds required in today's intense style of play.

Challenge your favourite grown-up and find out which of you is the biggest Championship brain!

ADULTS

Prior to moving to the Madejski Stadium, where did Reading play their home matches?

11 ANSWER

Which kit manufacturer produces Queens Park Rangers' 2020/21 playing strip?

12 ANSWER

At which Championship club did Preston goalkeeper Declan Rudd begin his career?

13 ANSWER

What nationality is Millwall goalkeeper Bartosz Bialkowski?

14 ANSWER

At which club did Coventry City manager Mark Robins begin his managerial career?

15 ANSWER

Who did Garry Monk succeed as Sheffield Wednesday boss in 2019?

16 ANSWER

What was the name of Derby County's former ground?

17 ANSWER

Cardiff City midfielder Will Vaulks plays international football for which country?

18 ANSWER

Who is the captain of Stoke City?

19 ANSWER

From which club did Preston North End sign Scott Sinclair?

20 ANSWER

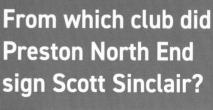

V KIDS

The adults' questions are on the left page and the kids' questions are on the right page.

ANSWERS ON PAGE 62

Who is the manager of Reading?

11 ANSWER

Freddie Woodman plays for which Championship club?

12 ANSWER

With which country is Norwich goalkeeper Tim Krul a full international?

13 ANSWER

Which club's nickname is 'The Lions'?

14 ANSWER

Which country did Stoke City manager Michael O'Neill guide to finals of Euro 2016?

15 ANSWER

What nationality is Norwich City manager Daniel Farke?

16 ANSWER

Roary the Lion is the official mascot of which Championship club?

17 ANSWER

Queens Park Rangers are famous for playing in what type of shirts?

18 ANSWER

Which Championship team play their home matches at Ewood Park?

19 ANSWER

Who is the manager of Rotherham United?

20 ANSWER

BOYS OF 1996

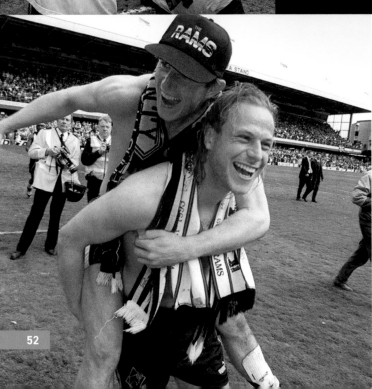

Jim Smith capped off a memorable first season at the Baseball Ground as Derby County finally reached the Premier League promised land.

The Rams had in fact made a rather uninspiring start to the 1995/96 campaign under new their manager Jim Smith and had just four wins in their opening 15 leagues games. However, they found a real level of consistency come the turn of the year and went into their final home game of the season with all to play for.

With Sunderland having already secured promotion, there was still one automatic promotion place remaining up for grabs and such was the standing in the league table that Smith's side went into their penultimate fixture knowing that victory would send them up.

IGOR STIMAC
STAR PERFORMER

Jim Smith's decision to invest £1.5M in Croatian centre-back Igor Stimac at the end of October 1995 proved to be a masterstroke and something of a turning point in the Rams' 1995/96 campaign.

Purchased from Hajduk Split, Stimac produced a number of quality performances at the heart of the Derby defence as Smith's side saw their promotion dream become a reality.

A hugely impressive character both on and off the pitch, Stimac spent almost four years at Derby County and represented his country in both Euro '96 and the 1998 World Cup finals in France. During the club's 125th anniversary celebrations in 2009 he was voted into the club's greatest all-time team.

In almost a Play-Off final environment but within the standard league programme, second-placed Derby took on third-place Crystal Palace with a four-point lead over the South London club - a Rams win and they were up. However, should the Eagles land all three points then it would have all headed down to the final game of the season away to West Bromwich Albion.

Once the action got underway, Derby enjoyed the perfect start as Dean Sturridge scored inside three minutes. This was to be no Sunday afternoon stroll though as Palace quickly equalised through Kenny Brown and the first half ended 1-1. Robin Van der Laan then became the toast of the Baseball Ground as the Dutchman headed the Rams back in front after 66 minutes.

Scenes of euphoria greeted the final whistle as Derby sealed second spot behind champions Sunderland, while Palace were left to face the Play-Off lottery.

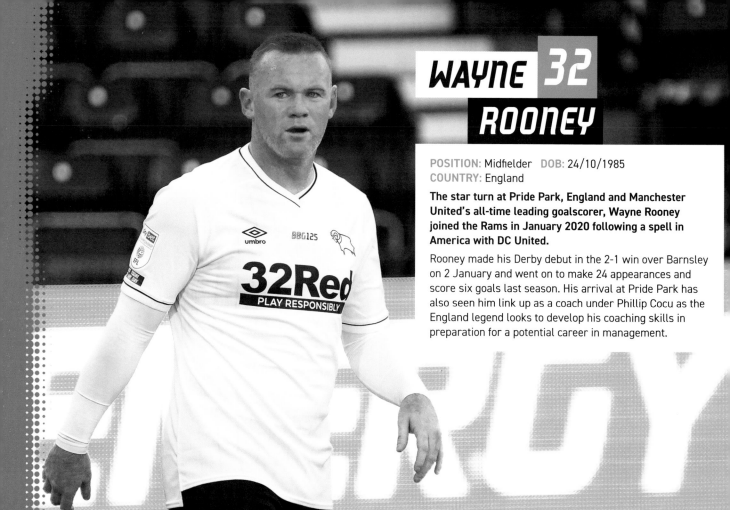

WAYNE 32 ROONEY

POSITION: Midfielder **DOB:** 24/10/1985
COUNTRY: England

The star turn at Pride Park, England and Manchester United's all-time leading goalscorer, Wayne Rooney joined the Rams in January 2020 following a spell in America with DC United.

Rooney made his Derby debut in the 2-1 win over Barnsley on 2 January and went on to make 24 appearances and score six goals last season. His arrival at Pride Park has also seen him link up as a coach under Phillip Cocu as the England legend looks to develop his coaching skills in preparation for a potential career in management.

33 CURTIS DAVIES

POSITION: Defender **DOB:** 15/03/1985
COUNTRY England

A vastly experienced member of the Rams' squad, 35-year-old defender Curtis Davies had played over 500 career games since first bursting onto the scene with Luton Town in 2003.

Very much the model professional, Davies made 37 appearances for the Rams in all competitions last season and proves to be a real role model for the club's younger players. He joined the Rams in the summer of 2017 and is closing in on a century of games for the club.

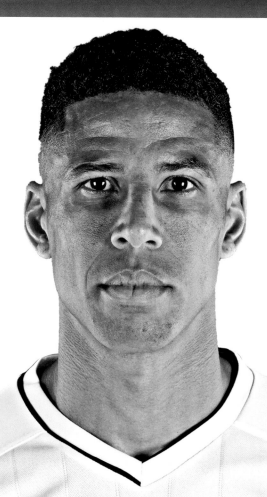

TEAM 2020/21

JASON 38 KNIGHT

POSITION: Midfielder   **DOB:** 13/02/2001
COUNTRY: Republic of Ireland

Midfielder Jason Knight was given his first taste of professional football when he debuted in the Rams' opening game of the 2019/20 campaign – a 2-1 win away to Huddersfield Town.

The Republic of Ireland under-21 international then proceeded to make 35 appearances in all competitions under Phillip Cocu last season. Knight also weighed in with six goals in his breakthrough campaign including a brace in the 2-1 home win over Charlton Athletic in December 2019.

JARGON BUSTER

Here is a list of footy jargon. All but one of the terms are hidden in the grid... can you work out which is missing?

All To Play For

Back Of The Net

Bags Of Pace

Big Game Player

Box-To-Box

Class Act

Derby Day

Dinked In

Early Doors

Funny Old Game

Game Of Two Halves

Handbags

Hat-Trick

Hollywood Pass

Keep It Tight

Massive Game

Midfield General

Natural Goalscorer

Row Z

Worldy

```
A S M Z U C E M A G E V I S S A M
V A W T B X O W A C V T S V Y B N
P O I B Y D I N K E D I N B R Q A
R L Q C J K X Z E F M L F J N E T
O G F W K C I R T T A H C S A Z U
E X B H D A V A P N H X G B J E R
T K A L L T O P L A Y F O R D C A
I R C P M E Q M O L R X G H O A L
F L K D N U R A S T T P K Q C P G
U F O N Z Y D I W O M W Y I B F O
N H F W Z O E S B B U N E H L O A
N J T G O B N O D F F X K A D S L
Y Z H S V R X M A G V O R N I G S
O X E A D C L H H G A E U D Z A C
L B N K Q Z L D C J N K A B I B O
D D E R B Y D A Y E E S P A L B R
G W T E U O I P G J I O J G S M E
A C I O K I R D Y U X K T S F A R
M H W V Y B L T B P C H F O R R A
E O P C D E E T G E G Q B L P E N
V G C M I H A F M I E K Y V Z G L
H J B F D W A R T X I D H D C T D
L X D M O A S T A S O L G A T C R
V I A Q K Y I H S O D W J H Y A Q
M P F E Z P R G R G U N F M I S G
Z I N Q E J N S L J P I K Z Y S O
D B S E V L A H O W T F O E M A G
A E K T X S L T E M X K W U L L I
S U S N Q L U W E A B V R S P C O
T A Y O R S F I T W Y O T A N B M
B H O L L Y W O O D P A S S U T I
```

MAX
BIRD

Want to leap like David Marshall, have the strength of Curtis Davies or boast the endurance of Jason Knight? Build up your strength for action with our...

30 DAY

Day 1
Right let's get started! 10 squats, 25 star jumps, 10 sit-ups - all before school!

Day 2
Make your mum a brew before going out to practice your keepy-uppies

Day 3
10 squats
50 star jumps
10 sit-ups

Day 4
How about swapping the crisps in your lunchbox for an apple?

Day 5
Take a one mile ride on your bike

Day 6
75 star jumps
15 sit-ups
15 press-ups

Day 7
Help clean the car before going out to play headers and volleys with your friends

Day 8
75 star jumps
15 sit-ups
15 press-ups
Before and after school now!

Day 9
Walk to school rather than take the bus

Day 10
Head to the swimming pool for a 30-minute swim

Day 11
100 star jumps
20 sit-ups
20 press-ups
Twice a day now, don't forget!

Day 12
Make sure you trade one of your fizzy drinks for a glass of water today

Day 13
Jog to the shop for your mum... before playing any video games!

Day 14
Give a hand around the house before kicking your ball against the wall 500 times

Day 15
Time to increase those exercises!
25 squats
25 sit-ups
25 press-ups
Before and after school!

Day 16
Take a nice paced two-mile jog today

Day 17
25 squats
150 star jumps
25 press-ups
Remember, before and after school

Day 18
Cycle to school rather than rely on the bus or a lift

Day 19
30 squats
150 star jumps
30 press-ups
Twice a day too!

Day 20
Get out and practice those free-kicks, practice makes perfect remember...

Day 21
Get peddling! Time for a two-mile trip on two wheels today

Day 22
Upping the workload now...
40 squats, 40 sit-ups
40 press-ups
Before and after school!

Day 23
Wave goodbye to the chips - ask for a nice salad for lunch today

Day 24
40 squats
40 sit-ups
40 press-ups
Twice a day, don't forget...

Day 25
Time to get pounding the streets - the jogging is up to three miles today

Day 26
45 star jumps
45 sit-ups
45 press-ups

Day 27
Time to swap those sweets and biscuits for some fruit

Day 28
45 star jumps
45 sit-ups
45 press-ups

Day 29
You're getting fitter and fitter now! Keep up the squats and star jumps plus join an after-school sports club - ideally football!

Day 30
Well done - you made it!
50 squats, 50 sit-ups and 50 press-ups!
These are the core ingredients to your success

CHALLENGE
to improve your all-round footy fitness!

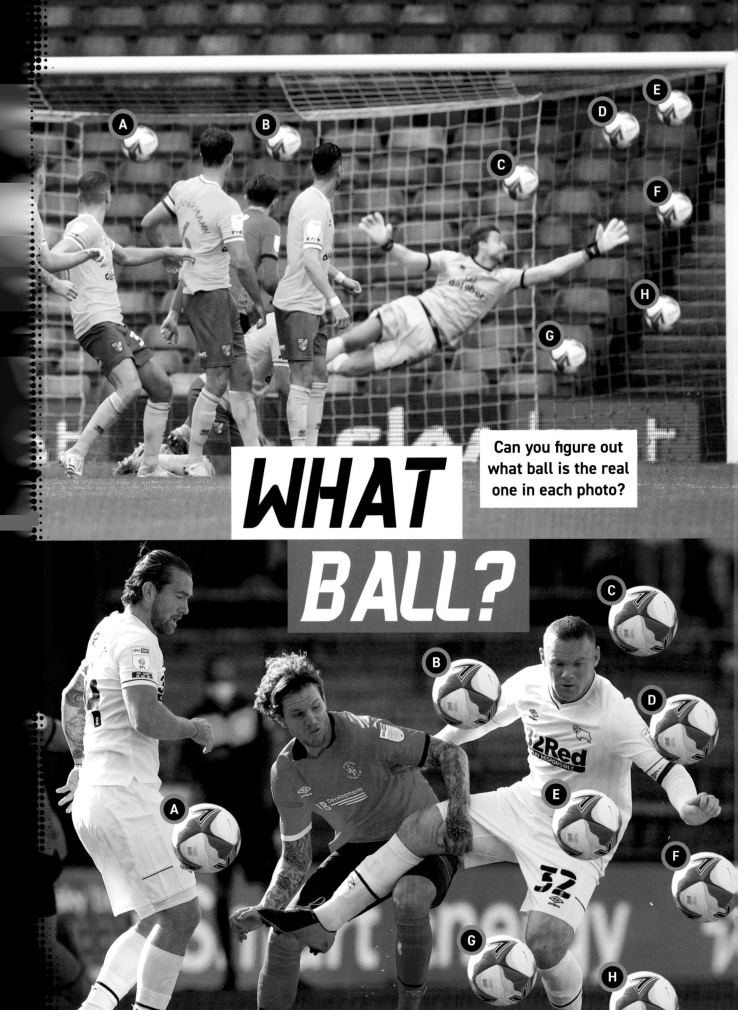

WHAT BALL?

Can you figure out what ball is the real one in each photo?

ANSWERS ON PAGE 62

NATHAN BYRNE

ANSWERS

PAGE 16 · ADULTS V KIDS

Adults

1. Blackburn Rovers. 2. Seven - Brentford, Bristol City, Luton Town, Millwall, Preston North End, Rotherham United and Wycombe Wanderers. 3. Jonny Howson. 4. Glasgow Rangers. 5. Middlesbrough. 6. Swansea City. 7. Nottingham Forest. 8. False. 9. Deepdale, Preston North End. 10. 2019.

Kids

1. Norwich City. 2. The Owls. 3. Coventry City and Rotherham United. 4. Bristol City. 5. Neil Harris. 6. Two, Cardiff City and Swansea City. 7. QPR. 8. Hillsborough, Sheffield Wednesday. 9. Seven - Birmingham City, Bristol City, Cardiff City, Coventry City, Norwich City, Stoke City and Swansea City. 10. Scottish.

PAGE 20 · WHO ARE YER?

1. George Evans. 2. Nathan Byrne.
3. Duane Holmes. 4. Kamil Jóźwiak.
5. David Marshall. 6. Andre Wisdom.
7. Morgan Whittaker. 8. Max Bird.
9. Graeme Shinnie. 10. Wayne Rooney.

PAGE 40
CLASSIC FANTASTIC →

PAGE 43
SPOT THE DIFFERENCE →

PAGE 50 · ADULTS V KIDS

Adults

11. Elm Park. 12. Errea. 13. Norwich City.
14. Polish. 15. Rotherham United. 16. Steve Bruce. 17. The Baseball Ground. 18. Wales.
19. Ryan Shawcross. 20. Celtic.

Kids

11. Veljko Paunović. 12. Swansea City.
13. Holland. 14. Millwall. 15. Northern Ireland.
16. German. 17. Middlesbrough. 18. Blue and white hoops. 19. Blackburn Rovers. 20. Paul Warne.

PAGE 56 · JARGON BUSTER

Big Game Player.

PAGE 60 · WHAT BALL?

TOP: Ball D.
BOTTOM: Ball F.